Little Stars

Little Stars
RODEO

A CRABTREE SEEDLINGS BOOK

Taylor Farley

CRABTREE
PUBLISHING COMPANY
WWW.CRABTREEBOOKS.COM

I love to go to the **rodeo**!

2

I wear my cowboy hat and boots.

I watch **bronc riding**.

I watch **barrel racing**.

But bull riding is my favorite **event**.

Rodeo clowns help out when riders fall.

rodeo clowns

Rodeo clowns are also called bullfighters.

I **compete** in the mutton bustin' event.

I wear a helmet and a **protective** vest.

helmet

protective vest

I hold on tight as long as I can!

Glossary

barrel racing (BA-ruhl RAYSS-ing): In barrel racing, a horse and rider race around three barrels in a cloverleaf pattern. The fastest horse and rider win.

bronc riding (BRONK RYE-ding): In a bronc riding event, a rider tries to stay on a bucking horse for eight seconds. The rider may only use one hand to hold the reins.

compete (kuhm-PEET): To compete is to try hard to win a contest against others.

event (uh-VENT): An event is a contest.

protective (pruh-TEKT-iv): Protective clothing helps keep us from getting hurt.

rodeo (ROH-dee-oh): A rodeo is a contest in which cowboys and cowgirls show their riding and roping skills.

Index

School-to-Home Support for Caregivers and Teachers

Crabtree Seedlings books help children grow by letting them practice reading. Here are a few guiding questions to help the reader build his or her comprehension skills. Possible answers are included.

Before Reading

- **What do I think this book is about?** I think this book is about the rodeo. It might tell us about different rodeo events.

- **What do I want to learn about this topic?** I want to learn about different rodeo animals. I see a sheep on the cover. What other animals are in the rodeo?

During Reading

- **I wonder why...** I wonder why rodeo clowns are also called bullfighters.

- **What have I learned so far?** I learned that there are horses, bulls, and sheep in the rodeo.

After Reading

- **What details did I learn about this topic?** I learned that rodeo events can be dangerous! A child can wear a helmet and a vest to stay safe.

- **Write down unfamiliar words and ask questions to help understand their meaning.** I see the word *compete* on page 16 and the word *protective* on page 18. The other vocabulary words are listed on pages 22 and 23.

Library and Archives Canada Cataloguing in Publication

Title: Little stars rodeo / Taylor Farley.
Other titles: Rodeo
Names: Farley, Taylor, author.
Description: Series statement: Little stars | "A Crabtree seedlings book". | Includes index. |
  Previously published in electronic format by Blue Door Education in 2020.
Identifiers: Canadiana 20200379755 | ISBN 9781427129833 (hardcover) | ISBN 9781427130013 (softcover)
Subjects: LCSH: Rodeos—Juvenile literature.
Classification: LCC GV1834 .F37 2021 | DDC j791.8/4—dc23

Library of Congress Cataloging-in-Publication Data

Names: Farley, Taylor, author.
Title: Little stars rodeo / Taylor Farley.
Other titles: Rodeo
Description: New York, NY : Crabtree Publishing Company, [2021] | Series: Little stars: a Crabtree seedlings book | Includes index.
Identifiers: LCCN 2020049428 | ISBN 9781427129833 (hardcover) | ISBN 9781427130013 (paperback)
Subjects: LCSH: Rodeos--Juvenile literature.
Classification: LCC GV1834 .F37 2021 | DDC 791.8/4--dc23
LC record available at https://lccn.loc.gov/2020049428

Crabtree Publishing Company

www.crabtreebooks.com   1–800–387–7650

e-book ISBN 978-1-949354-41-6

Print book version produced jointly with Blue Door Education in 2021

Written by Taylor Farley
Production coordinator and Prepress technician: Samara Parent
Print coordinator: Katherine Berti

Printed in the U.S.A./012021/CG20201102

Photo credits: Cover © Victoria Rak; page 2-3 © Amy K. Mitchell; page 5 © Jeanne Provost; page 6 © Amy K. Mitchell; page 8 © Kobby Dagan; page 11 © Centrill Media; page 12-13 © Jack Dagley Photography; page 14 © Shawn Hine; pages 17, 18, © Kobby Dagan
All photos from Shutterstock.com

Published in Canada
Crabtree Publishing
616 Welland Ave.
St. Catharines, Ontario
L2M 5V6

Published in the United States
Crabtree Publishing
347 Fifth Ave.
Suite 1402-145
New York, NY 10016

Published in the United Kingdom
Crabtree Publishing
Maritime House
Basin Road North, Hove
BN41 1WR

Published in Australia
Crabtree Publishing
Unit 3 – 5 Currumbin Court
Capalaba
QLD 4157